I0266547

The River of Perpetual Departure

The River of Perpetual Departure

Poems

Connie Johnstone

Cover design by Shay Culligan
Cover image by Mary Sand
Author photo by Jean Biegun

ISBN: 978-1-63980-774-1
Library of Congress Control Number: 2025946814

Kelsay Books
502 South 1040 East, A-119
American Fork, Utah 84003
Kelsaybooks.com

for my son, Charles Auen Warloe

Acknowledgments

The author gratefully acknowledges the editors of the following publications, in which these poems appeared previously:

Amethyst Review: "Leonard Cohen Sang to Me at Dawn"
The Brussels Review: "Mise-en-Scene," "Psalm One: Early Doubt Psalm"
The Calendula Review: "Envision This"
Ginosko Literary Journal: "Soirée at the Back Bay—*ars poetica*"
Loss: Anthology 9: "Women with Dead Husbands Have Questions"
The Orchards Poetry Journal: "Winter Relay"
Ravenous: le Terroir de Montolieu: "A Life of Rivers"
Spoon Knife Anthology, Numbers: "Counting On"
Tule Review: "Hell's Kitchen"
Voices 24: "Breath & Conversation"

The author would like to thank:

The late Kathryn Hohlwein—dear friend, mentor, spiritual guide. Jan Littman, there from the start with sustaining friendship and a great ear for authentic expression. Bob Stanley, Joyce Hsiao, and all the poets of Bob's Poetry Seminars, a writing and learning community that nurtures me and my work. Susan Kelly-DeWitt, mentor, friend, and inspiration. Mary Mackey, longtime mentor, writer, friend. Jan Haag, teacher, writer, friend. Jill Stockinger, friend, librarian-poet, reliable consultant. Jean Biegun, the Delta of Venus 5, and Dr. Andy Jones, who ushered me into the Davis poetry world where twice a month, on the roof or indoors, art listens at Natsoulas Gallery Poetry Nights. Sven Birkerts and Askold Melnyczuk, mentors at Bennington—writers, editors, teachers—whose example expanded my writing and my life. Rev. Bill Mark MDiv, Lorae Phelan MSNP BC, Donald Wexler MD—mentors at the Bedford VA Hospital PTSD Clinic—healers, mentors, storytellers, friends during my internship and beyond.

Contents

I. At the Headwaters

Soirée at the Back Bay—*ars poetica*

Perhaps no person can be a poet, or even can enjoy poetry, without a certain unsoundness of mind.
—Theodore Roethke, *The Poet's Business*

It's assumed that everyone has made a little effort. Make-up, some lipstick for women, a messy bun for those with longer hair. Beards trimmed on men, just a bit, and a surrendering look that says, yes, ok, this is a special night, the way men give their sleeves a tug upon entering. And the messy buns? Not that messy. We're young, in that mid-career way; we like looking at each other's residue of youth. But always included are those in late careers, to ground us all with gravitas and sense, to remind us that memory requires invitation, an intention for the evening's story to be told again, and thus all randomness and accident must be invited in. And most of us are arriving by subway, so, added vibration.

Outside in a courtyard the Euro-accented hostess and her Southern-accented husband seat us at their very long and rustic table. Food is served, candles are lit, fine wine is pouring. An artist stands, hands in pockets, beside his abstract painting on an easel, and describes his process of paint, newsprint, social comment. I stand, read an excerpt in progress, a conflicted Episcopal priest named Annie; my hands shake. A composer shares his new saxophone creation, a sound ribbon twirling through the leaves and shadows. Others read; someone sings.

We shrink in our seats when the famous poet of witness steps away from the table, then turns to face us and recite not read her poem, her latest excursion into international terror, leaving us with blood on our hands, feeling if we did not cause it, why were we not there? How does she do that?

After such brisk soul- and palate-cleansing, the husband stands and rings a little bell. The hostess bows her head, then tilts toward him, as he explains her furniture-artist work, a brief overview. She escorts us inside to see her creations. Watching their synchrony, one thinks about ballet, *pas de deux*. Our footsteps clatter on the polished floors.

Furniture pushed back against the walls. Rugs rolled up. Allowing for display. She is a maker of full-size chests and cabinets, two placed at the center, both recent winners of prestigious awards—wood smooth, silk-like. One stands on square legs, bleached birch, a shade of palest yellow. The other of polished mahogany, taller, on curved clawfoot legs. Each with fine, hair-thin traces of the grain. She says, "I hire a fabricator, but only when I must. I do love my electric planer." I like her voice, its deep, confiding register.

The husband leads us to framed, poster-size sheets of labyrinthine drawings like an electrical engineer's—her designs. All the little drawers and hinges. We are pulling tiny pegs on tiny chains from parts that open into other doors. What look like shelves hide compartments beneath them.

"Rubik's Cube," someone says. And then another says, "A giant jewelry box." Next one offers, "The Cabinet of Wonders, at the Met." Why do we keep comparing this to something else, I ask myself, but then I chime right in, "Alice, down the rabbit hole." Why do we want her to be the other, this furniture artist with her objects of intensity? Then I see the famous witness poet take the artist's hand. I notice the artist's short-clipped fingernails.

“You’ve externalized the pain, haven’t you?” How could she know to ask that? Conversely, how could I not have thought it? I must eavesdrop: “Not so much the pain,” the artist says, her brown eyes direct but also lowering as she speaks. “I’ve shown the places where it hides.”

She invites us to open the taller cabinet, discover hidden recesses, all of them cylindrical, she tells us, within the rectangular frame. On tiptoe I open a hinged lip on top and peek inside: a narrow mine-shaft tunnel where a tiny light flickers on or off; I feel a brief claustrophobic flash, I pull back.

I walk over by the courtyard doors, breathe. A noted editor, salt-and pepper man-bun, dark-rimmed glasses, comes over. “Art, the intricate world,” he says. Then, under his breath, “Hours and hours alone in a room.” Pascal, I think, uncertain. The hostess joins one man on hands and knees to see the cabinet undersides.

Reassembled at the table for dessert and coffee, some have questions: the time it took, when it all began. And was it lonely work? She laughs and says, “You need a little OCD to keep you company. And I am a perfectionist, you know.”

The man beside me sets down his mug of coffee; it thumps but doesn’t spill a drop. He’s a practicing psychiatrist who resembles Niles on Frasier; he also paints, is known to be on the spectrum. “OCD,” he declares, nodding as he speaks. “Obsessive Compulsive Disorder. That’s in the DSM. It isn’t normal.” He looks up.

Silence falls.

"Perfectionism." He rocks a little, side to side. "Also, in the DSM. Not normal." The editor leans across the table. "Grayson," he says. "Are not all artists hiding somewhere in the DSM?" A pause. Grayson is thinking.

Conversation is restarting, but with an undercurrent of significance, our minds turning inward, knowing now what to remember. At the subway station, the editor walks by and waves. I nod, complicit. He walks on down the stairs. I hop on the Green Line when it comes screeching in.

II. Wading In

Mise-en-Scene

We are born with the dead. They return and bring us with them.
—T.S. Eliot, *Little Gidding*

I was an idea of bright golden light.
My mother in labor, on ether, and telling a tale:
My father's young brother, the one she loved most,
blown up in explosions of German tank-guns.
I was an idea of bright golden light.
The nurses weep with her, a curtain of tears,
doctor attending with solemn regard.
War memories flood into each of their hearts.
I was an idea of bright golden light.
The audience waiting. My debut delayed.
My father in uniform, train running late.
Wet snow is clinging to his hair, to his coat.
I entered the world on that dark Christmas night.
My mother embraces him; I wave my hand.
They wrap me in blankets and carry me home.
A very old story is told once again, and again.

Psalm One: Early Doubt Psalm

Aunt Maggie's house was my favorite place to stay. Her canary, Thistle, lived in a white-painted cage in the kitchen, near wide windows overlooking the sea. Overnight, the cage was covered with tea towels; Thistle slept privately. She sang all morning, to sun or fog or ceiling. Early afternoons, the bird would stop, curl one foot around the wooden perch, lift the other leg and fold it up like landing gear. She might tuck her head beneath a wing, or not, but the gray lids closed, and for those moments the house held its breath: Thistle was resting. I was only three when visiting. Had I words, I would have said I'd come upon someone praying, holding safe some far-off space for us; if we deserved it, there was no saying.

Anthropology: Albuquerque Shards

> *An-thro-pol-o-gy* noun. *the systematic study of human societies and cultures and their development over time . . . examining lesser-known findings to reveal what was previously unknown or less fully understood.*
> —Oxford Language Dictionary

Red tile roof, sparrows' nests. Rough white stucco walls. Thorny pyracanthas, guardians on the porch. Tumbleweeds, backyard and sides. Anemic grass in front. Windows open out, with cranks. Inside walls are arched and white. The house my mother bought, Year Three AD. After the Divorce.

Her western jacket, suede and fringed. Year One, she wore it dancing. Her boyfriends and I shared mutual misunderstandings. My father's visits threw her off. She smashed her face in purple cushions she called the crying pillows. Sometimes, I did, too. Pink hollyhocks peeked in the kitchen, tried to cheer us up. I turned six. Punched several children. Sassed more than one adult. *We're both becoming feral,* she said. We left the rental house.

Adobe apartments. Oasis near the school. Teacher friends, all divorced, come by. Her best friend Betty has a daughter. Sandy's my same age. Girl Scout Camp together. Year Two AD. New Used piano. Gatherings, sing-alongs. I hear my mother playing Chopin, as I fall asleep. Bus for transportation. Lunch and movies after church. Milkman comes while we're at school, sets the bottles in the fridge. Kindness upon kindness shown. Next moving day: as soon as summer starts.

Year Three AD. Just three weeks in our new-old house. *We're going to paint the walls today,* she tells me early morning. Boxes in my room, still unpacked. New bunkbed feels like camp. Pinto beans simmer on the stove. She has me stirring cornbread batter. Triangular bandanas. Faded Levi's jeans. Friends arrive by nine a.m. It's Painting Day.

Sandy's read a new detective story; we play Murder in the tumbleweeds. And Ranch, out by the shed. And Tetherball, I have a brand-new pole. Chatter, laughter, shrieks and curses reach our ears outdoors. Sandy says it's otherworldly like her aunts in Ada, Oklahoma, on the porch.

They call us in for dinner on the table-shroud of sheets. Pinto beans and cornbread, bacon in the greens. Chocolate cake, thickly iced, matches walls just painted brown. Accent walls: some color called chartreuse. *You'll see,* my mother whispers, as she sees my eyes get wide. *We'll hang the leafy jungle curtains. Once the paint is dry.*

The sky goes dark. We stand out front, my mother's arm is draped across my shoulder. We wave and shout as friends depart. Squeeze quickly past the hulking pyracanthas. Screen door slaps shut all on its own, and we re-enter paradise, the jungle in the desert we call home.

Next time my father comes to take me for a visit, he takes one step inside. My mother tells him, *You can wait, over there, by the pyracanthas. She will be right out.* I turn nine. New rules apply. It's almost Four AD.

Half of Texas

"Half of Arizona
is blowing in from the west.
Half of Texas is
hurling sand at us
from the east,
and here we are
getting ourselves
sandpapered
saving this damn dog
because she woke up a
rattlesnake
that got too much rain
in its hole
and slithered out
on a rock
to dry out
in the wind,
and that rain was probably
rain
that should have
waited
till the hot days of August
for the god damned monsoon season,
and let the dust storms
come as scheduled
in the spring.
It's all right, girl,
I cut you
a good V there on your leg
and now
we'll just get you to the vet."

That was Jake, my mother's new husband,
who proceeded
to grunt and lift
into his mud-colored
Studebaker our notoriously
overweight old dog
who had faithfully followed
five of us from
the neighborhood out to
the arroyos that were just
drying up from rain,
and turning into glop
with all that newly imported
sand we'd felt a need
to see and touch, I guess.

The dog did live
to see other dog days.

But that Jake, he could make
everyone and everything
feel guilty
for the worldwide,
possibly interplanetary
conspiracy
aiming
to cause him distress.

Yet in 1973 he was
the Prophet of the Desert

in his way
because
what he was
calling out
that windy day,
what he had
every reason
to expect but was
not seeing:
the seasons
rotating
in an orderly
way.

He's been gone
these many years now,
but sometimes
I wonder,
sitting out here
in my lawn chair
after midnight
in my nightclothes
drinking my melted-ice
iced tea, trying to
cool off
after another day
under the heat dome,
I do ask myself,
What would Jake say now?

Down Home Easter Dinner, Southwest Style

If we were meant to change, we would not be who we are.
—Flannery O'Connor, "The Violent Bear It Away"

Gravel crunched underfoot as we made our way outside. We gathered at that homemade seven-foot-round dining table, in the shade of the lean-to patio cover. Mint jelly grew in cacti, the ceramic saguaro ones with serving arms. Leg of lamb hopped out of the oven trailing aromatics, rosemary sprigs, cilantro. Harmless trees of broccoli waited brightly green in serving bowls. Grasshopper pie and ice cream floats were chilling in the freezer. Our guest that year was the preacher, the rotund Reverend Taylor. Dressed in cowboy hat and Tony Lamas, he stood to tell a little story we would soon forget, and then he prayed, remembering Jesus who had risen from the dead. When he sat down, the chair cracked like a tree being axed and dropped him to the ground. My mother came to hover over the fallen preacher, the corners of her mouth aquiver. Her second husband Jake escaped through the backyard gate, lest his slapstick sense of humor get him in trouble. Uncle John was slightly tipsy, already tippling in the red wine and the white, but we would all remember it was him, veteran of the War, who had presence of mind and heart to bring a kitchen chair for the Reverend once they got him up. The rest of us were busy in our minds, composing this, the story we'd be telling into the next century. *What was it? Not innocence*—Every one of us so much ourselves in that minute.

Descendants

Circe took her time with Odysseus. She knew her powers,
whereas we were just discovering ours. We were never
more than 50 minutes from the Girls bathroom mirrors.

Did we fear we'd disappear between Algebra and World
Literature? We raced to get a look, confirmation
we had not reverted, during class, to last year's selves.

Circe took her time with Odysseus. She knew she had him,
whereas we were rushing to hallway postings on siren rocks
and crashing waves outside Rudy Miller's Geometry class

with no idea what we were going to do, when we hooked
our prey—Turn them into pigs or let them go? Circe did both,
catch and release. We did, too, but later, less easily, less divinely.

Winter Relay

Santa Fe National Forest, Semester Break, a January night. Three camper-mystics cocooned in down and wool, we stare at stars blinking at us in a black-ice sky. Impossible to submit to sleep, we keep our eyes on them, try choosing one and can't, keep blinking back: *Tag. You're it.* Exploration into vastness and minute detail, this trippy high-altitude encounter with extremes of scale. *Them/Us. Here/There.* In the car coming back, our weary voices continue, trying to tell each other how it felt, what it meant. I go still, silenced by a glance out the window. Geese, a flicker of wings, align in two dark vees, charcoal silhouettes across the rusted glow of sunset. How they are just going about their business. How stars are going about their billion-miles-away business. In magnificent delay, their light beams reached our retinas. With intention, we traveled to meet them. *Minute by minute. Laws of Attraction. Gravitational Pull.* That night, that sky, those stars. Forever with me should I ever wonder where I fit.

Scatter Math

We must have had a sense. Calls after midnight, more intense. Scattered time zones. Little sleep, with babies. Interfering parents. Striving husbands. Reagan president. Angsty phone calls. Carver stories. Didion essays. Malaise, expressed. Our own work, scratched on scraps. Read aloud. Typed up later. Onion skin with carbons. Mailed. Editors never answered. The best calls: always 3 a.m. Mine to Dorothy's New York 6 a.m. Carol's Santa Fe to my 2 a.m. Muddy mix of tears, subversive laughter. Sharing all. —Now a refutation comes. All these years later. In the Dictionary of Obscure Sorrows: *Sonder*. Each life is so complex. No one tells it total. Neither snail nor robin, nor the neighbor who calls the suicide hotline, weekly. Each of us a book never quite read through. I beg to disagree. Whispering voice, in a sleepy ear. *I know it's three. I had to call anyway*. Put aside your sonder. We knew our measure. Always a pattern, direct correlation. We told it all. In pieces.

Kiiko

For Stephen

Do colors want to be words? I see a color I think a word. I think yellow I think of you. My words feel worn and shabby, though. Yellow deserves better. So do you. I will use the Japanese word for yellow: *kiiko.* Already the air feels fresher when I send one breath of *kiiko* to you. I exhale light as bright as lemons.

Next thing I know, you're here like you were before darkness overtook you, your kiiko hair sun-glittering, small hands holding driftwood twigs. Kneeling beside the snow-melt water of the river we can never tiptoe in again, we sand-write the word for yellow. We write *kiiko*. Two characters: One for me. One for you.

Psalm Three: Sierra Psalm for Rocks

Blessed be the rocks and stones. The way they wait and move and break. Form with time and pressure. Store the warmth of days.

Blessed be the boulders at the canyon's rim where a marmot sat late this autumn afternoon—I was hiking & came upon the scene.

Its back pressed straight against a granite slab, front paws tucked, face lifted to slanting sun, cradled by a boulder's heat, beneath.

I stopped breathing, sent word to the holy one: I could die now and be complete. But breath returned and I walked on.

III. Caught in the Rapids

Women with Dead Husbands Have Questions

Some answers are provided them, at first. Obviously.
They know, now, how their marriages will end.
And when.

    Love can live forever or die, but marriages? They end,
    one way or another.

At home, later, when they look in the mirror, they say,
Oh, I am not a married woman, often still wearing
their wedding ring and, quite possibly, his, on a thumb.

    Who am I, then? But that's later.

Arguments with Death make no sense, but women with
dead husbands change position, drop their pleading arms,
lower their weeping eyes, direct their questions to the corpse.

    How could you do this? Die, they mean.
    Be dead, they mean. There's no quick comeback,
    no defensiveness, not even a shaky alibi.

It's disorienting, no one to argue against.

    Or lean against. Faced with the silence of one-way
    arguments,
    looking upon the bulk and muscularity of the unmoving
    male body, the next question these women might ask,

Who? Who am I going to lean against?
Leaning. Its meaning built on a foundation
of flirting. Leaning into. Tipsy in bars.

Then leaning down, to say Yes, when he knelt, to propose.
Leaning back against him, in a nursery peering down at
babies they've made. Leaning toward. Leaning on.
For support. Flashes of all that leaning. Gone.

Look at those shoulders. Those hands. Those fingers.
I paid extra for all the gold to go around your meaty
finger. Where do I put it now, the ring?

Touching the body mass, cradling the size-Large head, stroking
the long leg bones of a dead male, can make women with dead husbands say,

How can all of you, your entirety, be dead.

Envision This

She asks you to envision what she sees
under the microscope; do not be fooled.
There is more to this than she admits.

But take a look, through the lens of her description:
three one-celled mouse fibroblasts
—embryos divided before they can divide themselves—
seen in differing triangularity,
one true to form, one more circular, one stretched out.

Actin filaments, pick-up sticks scattered and stained red,
know their places, defining outer edges.
Speckled-blue DNA clusters hover at each center,
appear as if they might slip out, were they not held in,
by glowing green sticky-gel bumper cushions,
the fluorescent mitochondria.

She claims
these cellular creations emit auras of interrupted energy.
Improvisational artworks in a chalkboard blackness,
begun before eyes arrived, meant to be continued,
now caught in a micro-event
between ravenous eyes and biological science.
It's not the science.
She peers down

into a remembered vision of herself under glass
with all her billion cells exposed,
the day she is saying the final goodbye to her beloved,
with the eyes of those who love her, watching.

She has to travel with his heavy ashes
from the bedroom to the car,
the watchers' eyes assessing her well-being as she passes by.
They catch her in their sights: her bent-over-the-urn
posture, her sleepless face turned away from them,
her arms around him trembling with desire not to be seen.

She wants one last walk alone, just the two of them,
through the garden and out to the car.
She explains to them what she really wants—
To drive away with him to Lost Coast Black Sand Beach
where once at dawn a doe brought her fawn
to their window to be seen.
To stand there with him, looking out to sea.

She walks the ashes out.
She straightens her back, looks up from the microscope.
Improvisation begins,
continues.

Counting On

I inventory things.
Your shirts for donation.
Your photographs for framing.

        One by One.

Roll Call proceeds at North Star Pond.

Canada geese honk to each other,
practice for their coming migrations.

Mallard hens cluck soft encouragements,
lead hatchlings into wavy lines on water.

Swainson's Hawk flies to the top of a Tallen tree,
announces its presence to my binoculars.

        Here. Here. Here.

Days stack up. I can count them as they slide away,
colliding like beads on an abacus.

        Click. Click. Click.

Today I'd planned to leave three water stones somewhere
        at North Star Pond.

Subtracted them from our garden collection.
    -Lost Coast Beach -Half Moon Bay -Jenner's Cove
Then I brought them home again.
    +Jenner's Cove +Half Moon Bay +Lost Coast Beach
It felt like Addition.

This primitive arithmetic of the heart.
These beads of days, these stones I touch.

I have not achieved higher level mathematics.
    Algebra. Its name comes from the Arabic.
    Al-jabr. The reunion of lost parts.
    Where is X?

Still just counting.

Psalm Four: Sea Eagle Psalm for the Weary

The house I rented faced the beach at Pajaro. I drove in late, woke up early. Empty as the coffee cup beside me on the deck, I was nodding off, unread newspaper in my lap. Fog was backing up, headed out to sea. Mid morning on its way, already. Watching without seeing. All the birds out sweeping. Winging, dipping, diving, dancing. Along, above, near, far from the water. The changing angle of the sun forced me to move, a muscle or two. I rose from the chair, then sat down again. With my rising, a sea eagle must have broken from its rounds. A shadow crossed over. A thump, a weighted sound, occurred. I looked up. The bird perched on a beam extending from eaves, the power and exertion of flight still alive in the air around its feathers, brown and white and black on black. Flying, sweeping, dipping, diving—The bird is exhausted, I thought. I did not move. Winded, beak slightly open, it took a quick side-eye look at me. Fluffed its feathers, the slightest lift. Then the gray shade of its eyelid lowered like a cloud. I closed my eyes, received its blessing, offered mine. We shared our rest.

After His Death: Nomenclature, Redux

What if we named everything?. . . the way the reincarnated cry the most, bewildered by the star's second blink.
—Victoria Chang, *Today*

ONE

First time there, in seeming sleep of winter, she wants to meet with ones who watch birds. Brings binoculars, Audubon-approved. The ornithologist helps her view an adolescent Blue Heron who, though white right then, the expert tells her, later will turn blue. She sees the ess of its neck, and the tallow tree and the sky behind reflect on glassy water. She never joins the group, though. Finds facts and lenses are not the tools for her rebuilding.

TWO

Gray-brown winter gives way to lively chirping tweeting spring. All trees that can make color do so and become The Blossom Trees. She already knows their fluffy plum-crepe-myrtle-almond-cherry-tulip tree origins.

She names one loop of shore Goose's Beach Resort. Canada Geese motorboat, splashy wing propellers fanning. Show and Workout for thousand-mile flyers.

The Egret Inlet Conference Center she so dubs where Egrets endlessly study water that does, though rarely, ripple and flicker. They stare on patiently, until with sudden startling dip, they catch a fish.

She designates Pond's three sections Lungs: one the Dry Lobe, one the Manicured, and one the Wild Reserve, for ragged migratory birds like her who come and go. The Lobes all breathe together.

Gustav, heard-but-never-seen bull frog messenger, croaks from reeds and grasses eight feet tall. He takes vacation after autumn passes. Her ears play tricks, however. She hears Gustav every time she walks around the edges, like the voice of one you loved comes back in echoes, just because you want him to.

THREE

She seldom visits Pond for summer walks, cannot wake that early. But when she does at last show up, the music makers meet her. Songbirds cheep and chitter as she exits her air-conditioned car one quiet morning, air still soft before the heat can rise.

From a wooden viewing platform overlooking Goose's Beach Resort, she sees a Swainson's Hawk. He perches atop any tree he chooses. He keeps a distant watch. No need to name him since she knows him. She tells him thank you she can breathe now. She turns, though slowly, her footsteps sounding solid on the wooden planks and further on, solid still, on rock both decomposed and not.

Ode to a Black Bee

after Martin Heidegger

You were just one among the many bees
Assigned to pollinate the Palo Verde trees.

You looked like a bumble bee without yellow stripes.
Your legs had barbs, handy for hanging upside down
On yellow blossoms no bigger than my thumb.
You worked in tandem with golden honeybees,
Black beads, scattered jewels, high up in the yellow canopy.
Together you hummed from dawn to dusk, April to early June.
Every blossom got a visit, a revisit, as with zigzag flurries you
Withdrew the nectar and the pollen, to create the honey'd alchemy.

That morning in May, the buzzing, humming music called me.
You were on the ground beside the sitting wall, completely still,
You, a shiny black something, covered by yellow fallen blossoms.
I saw your one leg move and stop and then not move again.
Was it a breeze? Someone said bees rest and sleep inside of
flowers when they have a need . . . but no.

I sat with you. Expressed my admiration.
Asked you questions about just working, as living.
Needed your advice on just being, as belonging.
Reached down, touched your warm enclosure,
Then picked you up, placed you in my palm.
You were weightless.
I could not feel you in my hand.
Not like a feather. Not like paper.
Without weight.
Like vapor.

IV. Beyond the Riverbank

Leonard Cohen Sang to Me at Dawn

The dream was thrilling until
he stopped singing and,
like a zen master
presenting
a koan,
he said,
Song of praise.
I will think about that, I thought.
Then he declared, in a voice clear as ringing bells,
reflective as still water,
—*Sing! Sing a song of praise.*
I tried to protest in my sleep-dream
paralysis, tried to say: I. Can't. Sing.

But I was not the woman who could
say no to Leonard Cohen. I started
weeping, told him that life and
world of late were unholy and unfit
for any song or praise, for reasons I chose not
to enumerate. In the dream he knew
anyway. Into the lifting light of the
morning, Leonard Cohen

vanished, leaving trails of irony, throaty laughter,
a smell like moldy feathers and some eerie words
that echoed like a shameful scolding from a god
I used to know who loved the broken:
What else is there to sing of
if not the unholy holy?
As I awoke, I heard myself singing:

O planet spinning, blue and green.
O mother mine, her touch.
O fathers, in their time.
O muscles in my legs and arms.
O lovers and children.
O ancestors, friends.
O nurse.
O holy one.
All who will have carried me
to the finish line.
Ahead of time, I sing your praises.

I Respond to the Impossible Dilemma of Terrible Error

People you love show you scars, want answers.
Apologies are twirling, anorexic dancers.
—Autumn Newman, Manic Episode

In an Alice Munro story, I could always count on remedies
—old, Canadian, unfamiliar to me.

My wounds could not be plugged by reading The Albanian Virgin.
Paste made with beeswax, olive oil and pine resin
was not going to stanch the crying out my heart was doing.

But I could lie down in the *kula*—house of the sick and dying,
on a bed of freshly pulled ferns,
and, while in delirium, turn dirty-window spider webs into
black-lace curtains.

Is that how it was for Alice, too? That rooting out of remedy
for those of us who knew, as she knew, there was no undoing.

Dear Sir

Cento, variation

Dear Sir,

Into the dangerous world I leapt:

Pine trees like priests . . .
and madmen with crocus words ready to bloom
and the secret shelter of sparrow feathers fallen on the earth.
In me, scarlet-jacketed armies marched into rain.

And the god of rocks said, *Stop.*
The god of rocks his voice shale, the words, *Live Again,*
locked on his silent stone tongue.

The god of rocks said, *Stop.*
A kind of tinfoil-chewed shiver of the soul.

The god of rocks said, *Stop.*
And from beneath the the rust of years,
the place where he cried became holy.

Professors here in glass sneakers,
washing history off the shelves,
have passed with a nod of the head
or polite meaningless words.

With horror, sir,

Sincerely,

Lucile Adler, Agha Shahid Ali, William Blake, Yehoshua
November, Pattiann Rogers, Christian Wiman, James Wright,
William Butler Yeats, and I, your humble compiler.

Hell's Kitchen

Now that God is news, what's left but prayer?
—Agha Shahid Ali, "Rooms Are Never Finished"

In the basement room under the bakery on 47th Street,
she sits in yeasty silence in a circle with her sangha.

Holding cradle pose, heads down and turned, they rock
and feed starving Gaza babies, unsung lullabies rising.

Standing bent and leaning, searchlight pose, they sweep
lanterns, rescue Israelis in tunnels, dark air stirring.

Eyes screen-burned from watching second-hand and
third-hand horror, eardrums burst from words exploding,

they calm their minds in lotus pose. She climbs the stairs.
Baking scents swirl and cling, chase her in the street.

Bread smells of its own small deaths. But she will be back
in the morning, to buy the bread, breathe it and break it, eat.

How to Mend a Broken Soldier

As a man, lead knee to knee.
Sit with your legs spread,
Lean your shoulders toward him,
Look down, then lift your head.
He will hear you.

As a woman, lead face to face.
Lay your hands on the table,
Never look away.
Take a breath as you are able.
He will see you.

Ask him to tell you details of the befores.
The boy earned cash for sodas and fries
From Stan at the Texaco station,
Made of his attic room a sailor's watch
With telescope. His father drank too much.
Don't let the boy-before get lost
In the crossfire of the man
Who came after.

Offer him wordless ways to speak.
He'll look askance at crafty balsa wood,
Yet he'll erect the tower
Where his failed repairs
Scrambled signals. Deadly effects.
He will tell you that, and more.

Let his words pour, into your silence.
The CO chewed his 19-year-old ass, seemed like hours.
He'd killed his own. The dead came back.
Some were whole and some in pieces.
One day overpowers all.

For 20 years, his friend Jim Beam
Has told him, *Not to Worry*.

Take a chance. Ask him if he would like to write
As if his name were Barley Malone
Who went to war in a bucket of stones.
And, here. Take the Play-Doh home.
He sees your scheme. He grins.

The only Play-Doh used was army green,
A soldier figure on his knees.
Go ahead and wonder why.
Barley's clay, he'll say. He's the only one
That I can change. And, yeah, I know.
He's me.

He'll go on to write as Barley Malone,
Get his story told and then tell you:
He forgave Barley's sins,
And only then, his own.

Some call this process externalization.
Boomerang effect. His story comes back.

Not the same. Having lost some of its power
To hurt him.

There will be many ways to say goodbye.
This is one.

You will go with the chaplain
On a cold winter day
To bless the soldier's house,
And feast and pray.

The day will be ending,
Sun ready to set.
The soldier's wife and dog
will lie down with him
on a big wide bed.

They'll laugh, and bark and laugh again,
As the chaplain chants a prayer of peace,
Sprinkles holy water from a silver cup, and
Drops fall on their blinking eyes,
Their upturned smiling faces.

It's then you will walk away,
Just when you don't want to.
Some call it termination
Of care. You will remember
A celebration.

Breath & Conversation

The nurse's text:
End Stage Lung Disease. Despairing.
Disruptive. Needs your magic.

> "The nurse said she was going to call you."
> Standing by the window, he yanks
> the O^2 tubing like a leash.

Chaplain protocol: Ask open-ended questions.
Answers require air. I will use declarations:

"It gets so you hardly know yourself."

> "That's the goddam truth. I've had it."

His chart said Presbyterian. He might like hymns.

"I have Ave Maria, instrumental version."
I scroll right to its slow consoling rhythms.

He looks at me with rheumy eyes, expression unreadable.

Not all things are blessed.
I should have offered Amazing Grace.

> His chest inflates, shoulders pull back.
> He clears his throat and sings. In Latin.
> *Ave. Ave Dominu . . .* baritone.
> Loses a few notes, holds important ones.
> The music ends. He grips the windowsill.
> "I used to sing in choruses," he gasps.

Breathless with surprise, I declare,
> "You still do."

Unpacking

> *The Shona of Africa live with a sense of the dead among them, as continuing members of community . . . while other mourners create a new biography of the deceased, knowing them better by doing so.*
> —Tony Walter, *A New Model of Grief: The Living Integrate the Dead.* "Mortality," University of Bath, 1996

That day she carried grief like a satchel to work.

She had come in early to sit with a shrunken,
wrinkled man who had no next of kin and who
was making loud infrequent breathing sounds,
nearing-death slow music the nurses called
Cheyne Stoking.

Her voice became his barely known companion, as
she told him she was there, and that her niece was not.
A young beautiful woman who had gone and left
no forwarding address, taken so soon, leaving two
tiny children and her beloved here on earth.

Her voice continued softly on.

Sunlight now pouring in the window seemed to
make him squint, she told him. She went over
to adjust the blinds. Better, she whispered as
she sat back down, then blinked.

Her niece's face was floating, if not levitating,
if not arising out of his.

Smooth skin, thick eyebrows, full lips appeared in the
air, making invisible his hawkish nose, his skull
silhouette.

A moment's vision, then gone.
A haunting consolation, she thought, just like her
to want to help.

Her tears were not for him exactly, as she placed
a cool damp cloth on his dear forehead.
He sighed, a jagged kind of whimper that said
the rag did help, his grimace disappearing.

She took his hand. She closed her eyes.
She said a common prayer.

Over Time

. . . memories that make just one olive of time, like a hundred pelts
make one fur coat, like a thousand wounds make one newspaper article
—Guillaume Apollinaire, "Ombré"

He was a military man. Perhaps . . . you are his country now
—David L. Schiedermayer, MD, "Duty"

They sit here every morning
after breakfast,
looking out.

He keeps the windows open,
even when it rains.
She doesn't

notice hazy panes, dirt-rain
blends of wind,
but now

a bright red headscarf spins,
snags on thorny
tumbleweeds,

her synapses seem to fire,
he leans forward,
and she blinks

at him, says,
Kqrstrk! whatever
it means.

Her brief glance of
recognition stirs
vicious little

false-hope snippets in his head.
Over time, he has learned
a certain grace:

He bakes the moment
tender
in the kiln—

his reluctant
but accumulating
memory.

The thousand moments
weigh him
down,

but do not outweigh
his love
as yet,

though at times
her emptying
mind

can
make him
envious.

A Life of Rivers

More inward than sex or even womb, inmost in woman
is the girl, intact

—Ursula K. Le Guin, "Song"

Here I am being born in Charleston.
Along the muddy old Kanawha. All things old
were there. Made with time.
Like coal. Like my dear ancestors.
Their old love. It made me.
Here I am along the Missouri. Vocalizing morning
clucks of next-door pullets. Poking holes
in sunlit tree-shadow-sounds on
the ceiling. Earliest imagery.
Here I am by the Bitterroot.
Coyotes cry to stars. I dream
my mother floats into a glacier,
falls from a log. I keep my dream a secret.
Then tell the coyotes. Neutral audience
receives it
without comment.
The stars shine on.
Here I am at the Snake, feeding into Jackson Lake.
I leave my body at the edge, rinsing face
and hands before breakfast. I fly up
above the Tetons. A girl kneels by the river.
How tiny but how safe
she is, in the wordless
beauty of the world.
I return, soon smell bacon.
Here I am at the Rio Grande. Respite
under cottonwoods in sand.

Laundry flapping on a line.
Tiled-floor rooms. Thick-
walled Sanctuaries. Watercolor, oil,
and wood. I learn. Vicariously. The layered
life of making and being. Blended into one.
Here I am on the American.
Cold Sierra snow water, rapidly
descending. Quenching my thirst
for awhile. Cats snoozing.
Children's bicycles lounging,
against the house. Me, birthing,
words into books.
Here I am at the Charles. Crossing Longfellow's
Bridge, boats rowing below. A sense
of waiting. Slow turns. Currents shifting.
Neither crew, nor pilot.
No charts to go on. Exhilarating.
Here I am, walking along the Seine.
Midday in Paris.
Sachet bundles floating down
from rows of linden trees.
Everywhere the wisps
of wind. Wrists
going pale
in surrender. Only
light, only breathing.

Here I am, at the untamed river.
The one I've always traveled in,
the river of imagination, unnamed
but now christened. In the village Montolieu.
I ask for someone to say the river's name.
In French. Several consult. It is decided:
"Madame, your river is called
Le Rivière du Dèpart Ininterrompu."
The translation delights me. I continue
In this river of perpetual departure.

Notes

In my poem "Hell's Kitchen," the line *Bread smells of its own small deaths* comes from "All Bread" by Margaret Atwood.

The very loosely adapted term "Scatter Math" in my poem of the same name can be described as the relationship between variables plotted on a graph, allowing visualization of patterns.

Here are the source poems for "Dear Sir," my cento variation:
Lucile Adler: "With Horror, Sir, Sincerely" and "When the Decision Was Taken"
Agha Shahid Ali: "In Search of Evanescence"
William Blake: "Infant Sorrow"
Yehoshua November: "How a Place Becomes Holy"
Pattiann Rogers: "The Death of Living Rocks and the Consequences Thereof"
Christian Wiman: "Dark Charms"
James Wright: "Living by the Red River" and "I Was Afraid of Dying"
William Butler Yeats: "Easter 1916"

About the Poet

The River of Perpetual Departure is Connie Johnstone's first book of poetry. Her poems have appeared in many journals: *Amethyst Review; The Brussels Review; The Calendula Review; Comstock Review; Ginosko Literary Journal; Gyroscope; Loss: Anthology 9; The Orchards Poetry Journal; Ravenous: le Terroir de Montolieu; Paris: Great Cities Vol. 1; Spoon Knife Anthology: Numbers; Tule Review; Voices 24;* and others.

She published a novel, *The Legend of Olivia Cosmos Montevideo* (Atlantic Monthly Press) and edited an anthology, *I've Always Meant to Tell You* (Pocket Books). She was a professor of English/chair of creative writing at American River College; Hospice chaplain, Kaiser Permanente, specializing in Narrative Therapy. Degrees include MFA Bennington and MTS Harvard Divinity School. She is at work on a second book of poems, *Black Snake in a Bamboo Pole.*

www.ingramcontent.com/pod-product-compliance
Lightning Source LLC
Chambersburg PA
CBHW071012160426
43193CB00012B/2028
* 9 7 8 1 6 3 9 8 0 7 7 4 1 *